MW01198908

The

INITIATES

of the

FLAME

FULLY ILLUSTRATED

by

Manly Palmer Hall

𝕳e who lives the 𝕷ife shall know the 𝕯octrine

CONTENTS

ILLUSTRATIONS

The Initiates *of the* Flame

INTRODUCTION

ew realize that even at the present stage of civilization in this world, there are souls who, like the priests of the ancient temples, walk the earth and watch and guard the sacred fires that burn upon the altar of humanity. Purified ones they are, who have renounced the life of this sphere in order to guard and protect the Flame, that spiritual principle in man, now hidden beneath the ruins of his fallen temple.

As we think of the nations that are past, of Greece and Rome and the grandeur that was Egypt's, we sigh as we recall the story of their fall; and we watch the nations of today, not knowing which will be the next to draw its shroud around itself and join that great ghostly file of peoples that are dead.

But everywhere, even in the rise and fall of nations, we see through the haze of materiality, justice; everywhere we see reward, not of man but of the invincible One, the eternal Flame.

A great hand reaches out from the unseen and regulates the affairs of man. It reaches out from that great spiritual Flame which nourishes all created things, the never dying fire that burns on the sacred altar of Cosmos—that great fire which is the spirit of God.

If we turn again to the races now dead, we shall, if we look, find the cause of their destruction. **The light had gone out.** When the flame within the body is withdrawn, the body is dead. When the light was taken from the altar, the temple was no longer the dwelling place of a living God.

Degeneracy, lust, and passion, hates and fears, crept into the souls of Greece and Rome, and Black Magic overshadowed Egypt; the light upon the altar grew weaker and weaker. The priests lost the Word, the name of the Flame. Little by little the Flame flickered out, and as the last spark grew cold, a mighty nation died, buried beneath the dead ashes of its own spiritual fire.

But the Flame did not die. Like spirit of which it is the essence, it cannot die, because it is life, and life cannot cease to be. In some wilderness of land or sea it rested once again, and there rose a mighty nation around that flame. So history goes on through the ages. As long as a people are true to the Flame, it remains, but when they cease to nourish it with their lives, it goes on to other lands and other worlds.

Those who worship this Flame are now called heathens. Little do we realize that we are heathen ourselves until we are baptized of the Holy Spirit, which is Fire, for fire is Light, and the children of the Flame are the Sons of Light, even as God is Light.

There are those who have for ages labored with man to help him to kindle within himself this spark, which is his divine birthright. It is these who by their lives of self-sacrifice and service have awakened and tended this fire, and who through ages of study have learned the mystery it contained, that we now call the "Initiates of the Flame."

For ages they have labored with mankind to help him to uncover the light within himself, and on the pages of history they have left their seal, the seal of Fire.

Unhonored and unsung they have labored with humanity, and now their lives are used as fairy stories to amuse children, but the time will yet come when the world shall know the work they did and realize that our present civilization is raised upon the shoulders of the mighty demigods of the past. We stand as Faust stood, with all our lore, a fool no wiser than before, because we refuse to take the truths they gave us and the evidence of their experiences. Let us honor these Sons of the Flame, not by words, but by so living that their sacrifice shall not be in vain. They have shown us the way, they have led man to the gateway of the unknown, and there in their robes of glory passed behind the Veil. Their lives were the key to their wisdom, as it must always be. They have gone, but in history they stand, milestones on the road of human progress.

Let us watch these mighty ones as they pass silently by. First, Orpheus, playing upon the seven stringed lyre of his own being, the music of the spheres. Then Hermes, the thrice greatest, with his emerald tablet of divine revelation. Through the shades of the past we dimly see Krishna, the illuminated, who on the battlefield of life taught man the mysteries of his own soul. Then we see the sublime Buddha, his yellow robe not half so glorious as the heart it covered, and our own dear Master, the man Jesus, his head surrounded with a halo of Golden Flame, and his brow serene with the calm of mastery. Then Mohammed, Zoroaster, Confucius, Odin, and Moses, and others no less worthy pass by before the eyes of the student. They were the Sons of Flame. From the Flame they came, and to the Flame they have returned. To us they beckon, and bid us join them, and in our robes of self-earned glory to serve the Flame they love.

They were without creed or clan; they served but the one great ideal. From the same place they all came, and to the same place they have returned. There was no superiority there. Hand in hand they labor for humanity. Each loves the other, for the power that has made them masters has shown them the **Brotherhood** of all life.

In the pages that follow we will try to show this great thread, the spiritual thread, the thread of living fire that winds in and out through all religions and binds them together with a mutual ideal and mutual needs. In the story of the Grail and the Legends of King Arthur we find that thread wound around the Table of the King and the Temple of Mount Salvart. This same thread of life that passes through the roses of the Rosicrucians, winds among the pedals of the Lotus, and among the temple pillars of Luxor. THERE IS BUT ONE RELIGION IN ALL THE WORLD, and that is the worship of God, the spiritual Flame of the universe. Under many names He is known in all lands, but as Iswari or Ammon or God, He is the same, the Creator of the universe, and fire is His universal symbol.

We are the Flame-Born Sons of God, thrown out as sparks from the wheels of the infinite. Around this Flame we have built forms which have hidden our light, but as students we are increasing this light by love and service, until it shall again proclaim us Suns of the Eternal.

Within us burns that Flame, and before Its altar the lower man must bow, a faithful servant of the Higher. When he serves the Flame he grows, and the light grows until he takes his place with the true Initiates of the universe, those who have given all to the Infinite, in the name of the Flame within.

Let us find this Flame and also serve it, realizing that it is in all created things, that all are one because all are part of that eternal Flame, the fire of spirit, the life and power of the universe.

Upon the altar of this Flame, to the true creator of this book, the writer offers it, and dedicates it to the one Fire which blazes forth from God, and is now hidden within each living thing.

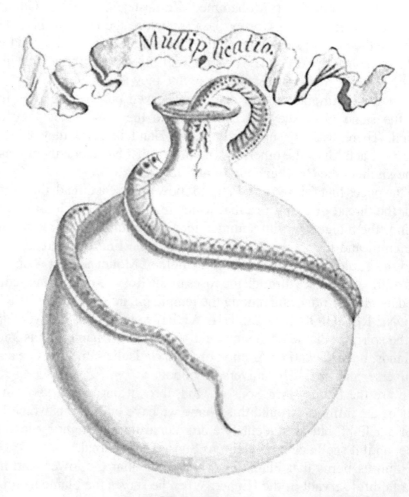

Multiplicatio.

FOREWORD

THE GREATEST OF MYSTERY SCHOOLS

he World is the schoolroom of God. Our being in school does not make us learn, but within that school is the opportunity for all learning. It has its grades and its classes, its sciences and its arts, and admission to it is the birthright of man. Its graduates are its teachers, its pupils are all created things. Its examples are Nature, and its rules are God's laws. Those who would go into the greater colleges and universities must first, day by day, and year by year, work through the common school of life, and present to their new teachers the diplomas they have won, upon which is written the name that none may read save those who have received it.

The hours may seem long, and the teachers cruel, but each of us must walk that path, and the only ones ready to go onward are those who have passed through the gateway of experience,

GOD'S GREAT SCHOOL FOR MAN

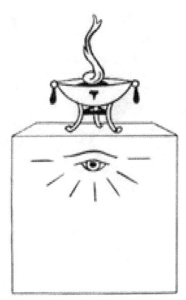

> **The Cube Altar:**
> *Of the elements of the earth is this altar composed. It is the great cube of matter. On or in this altar burns a Flame. It is this Flame that is the spirit of all created things.* **Man, know thyself.** *Thou art the Flame, and thy bodies are the living altar.*

Chapter I

The Fire Upon *the* Altar

s far back as our history goes we find that fire has played an important part in the religious ceremonial of the human race. In practically every religion we find the sacred altar fires, which were guarded by the priests and vestals with greater care than their own lives. In the Bible we find many references made to the sacred fires which were used as one form of devotion by the ancient Israelites. The Altar of Burnt Offerings is as old as the human race, and dates from the time when the first man, lifting himself out of the mists of ancient Lemuria, first saw the sun, the great Fire Spirit of the universe. Among the followers of Zoroaster, the Persian Initiate, fire has been used for centuries in honor of the great Fire God, Ormuzd, who is said by them to have created the universe.

> ### *The Ever-burning Lamp:*
> *Know that the Flame that burns within thee and lights thy way is the ever-burning lamp of the ancients. As their lamps were fed by the purest of oil, so thy spiritual Flame must be fed by a life of purity and altruism.*

There are two paths or divisions of humanity whose history is closely related to that of the Wisdom Teachings. They embody the doctrines of fire and water, the two opposites of nature. Those who follow the path of faith or the heart, use water, and are known as the Sons of Seth, while those who follow the path of the mind and action are the Children of Cain, who was the son of

Samael, the Spirit of Fire. Today we find the latter among the alchemists, the hermetic philosophers, the Rosicrucians, and the Freemasons.

It is well for us to understand that we ourselves are the cube altar upon which and in which burns the altar fire. For many centuries the Initiate of fire has been nourishing and guarding the Spiritual Flame within himself, as the ancient priests watched day and night the altar fires of Vesta's temple.

The ever-burning lamp of the alchemist, which having burned thousands of years without fuel in the catacombs of Rome, is but a symbol of this same spiritual fire within himself. In the picture we see the ever-burning lamp which was carried by the Initiate in his wandering. It represents the spinal column of man, at the top of which is flickering a little blue and red flame. As the lamp of the ancients was fed and kept burning by the purest of olive oil, so man is transmitting within himself and cleansing in the laver of purification the life essences, which, when turned upward, provide fuel for the ever-burning lamp within himself.

The Masonic Censor:
As the perfume rising from the incense burner was acceptable in the sight of the Lord, so may our words and actions ever be a sweet incense acceptable in the sight of the Most High.

Upon the altars of the ancients were offered sacrifices to their gods. The ancient Hierophant offered up sacrifices of spices and incense. The Masonic brother of today still has among his symbols the incense burner or censer, but few of the brothers recognize themselves in this symbol. The ancients symbolized under such things as this the development of the individual, and as the tiny spark burning among the incense cubes slowly consumes all, so the Spiritual Flame within the student is slowly burning away and transmuting the base metals and properties within himself and offering up the essence thereof as the smoke upon the altar of Divinity. It is said that King Solomon, when he completed his temple, offered bulls as a sacrifice to the Lord, by burning them upon the temple altar. Those who believe in a harmless life wonder why so many references are made in the Bible to animal sacrifice.

The student realizes that the animal sacrifices are those of the celestial zodiac, and that when the Ram or the Bull was offered upon the altar, it represented the qualities in man which come through Aries, the celestial Ram, and Taurus, the Bull in the zodiac. In other words, the Initiate, passing through his tests and purification, is offering upon the altar of his own higher being the lower animal instincts and desires within himself. Among the Masonic brothers we also find what is called the Symbol of Mortality. It is a spade, a coffin, and an open grave, while upon the coffin has been laid a sprig of acacia, or evergreen. In the picture we see the spade of the grave digger, which has been considered the symbol of death for centuries.

The Grave Digger's Spade:
Let us take the spade that now digs our grave through the passions and emotions of life and use it to unearth the secret room far below the rubbish of the fallen temple of the human soul.

In the Book of Thoth, that strange document which has descended to man at his present stage of evolution as a deck of playing cards, we find a very wonderful symbolism. Of all the suits of cards, that of the spade is the only suit in which all the court cards face away from the pip. In all the other kings and queens, the faces are looking at the little marker in the corner of the card, but in the spade suit, they look away from it. Now it is said that the spade has been taken from the acorn, but the occult student has a different idea. He sees in the spade, which has for ages been the symbol of death, a certain part of his own anatomy. If you will again turn to the picture of the spade, you will see, if you have ever studied anatomy, that the grave digger's spade is the spinal column, and the spade-shaped piece which is used on the deck of cards, is nothing more nor less than the sacrum bone.

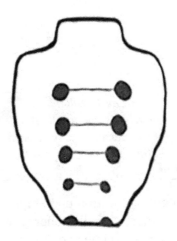

This bone forms the base of the spinal column, and is also the spear of the Passion. Through it and the foramana which pierce it, pass the roots of the spinal nerve, which indeed are the roots of the Tree of Life. It is the center through which are nourished and fed the lower vertebrae of the spine, and the sacrum and coxygeal bones that dig the graves for all created things. This point has been beautifully symbolized by the grave digger's spade, which has been used by the brothers of many mystic organizations for ages. The currents and forces working through these lower spinal nerves must be transmuted and lifted upward to feed the altar fire at the positive or upper end of the spine.

The Candle:
This is the light that has gone out. It is the candle that is hidden under the bushel.
This is the true light that forever dispels the darkness of ignorance and
uncertainty. Let the light shine forth through a purified body and
a balanced mind. For this light is the life of our brother creatures.

The centering of thought or emotion upon higher or lower things, as the case may be, determines where thin life energy will be expended. If the lower emotions predominate, the flame upon the altar burns low and flickers out, because the forces which feed it have been concentrated upon the lower centers. But when altruism predominates, then the lower forces are raised upward and pass through the purification which makes possible their being used as fuel for the ever-burning lamp. Thus, we see why it was a great sin to let the lamp go out, for the pillar of flames which hovers over the Tabernacle, purified and prepared after the directions of the Most High, is the Spiritual Flame that, hovering above man, lights his way wherever he may go.

The sun of our solar system, that is, the Spiritual Sun behind the physical globe, is one of these Flames. It began no greater than ours, and through the power of attraction and the transmuting of its ever-increasing energies it has reached its present proportions. This flame in man is the "light that shineth in darkness." It is the Spiritual Flame within himself. It lights his way as no exterior light can. This radiating out from him brings into view, one by one, the hidden things of the cosmos, and his ignorance is dispelled in exactly the same proportion as his light is spread, for the darkness of the unknown can only be removed by light, and the greater the light, the further back the darkness is driven. This is the Lamp of the Philosopher, which he carries through the dark passageways of life, and by the light of which he walks among the stones and along the narrow cliff edge without fear. But although he gain all other things and have not this light within himself, he cannot know where he goes; he cannot watch his footsteps; and he cannot dispel his ignorance with the light of truth.

Therefore let each student watch the fire that burns upon his altar. Let him also make that altar, his body, as beautiful and harmonious as possible, and let him also sacrifice upon that altar the frankincense and myrrh, his actions and his deeds. As in the Tabernacle he offers all upon the altar of divinity, so let him day by day dispel the symbols of mortality—the coffin and the open grave by which he prepared himself through the mastery of the lower emotions within himself—and recognize that no matter how crystallized or dead his life may be, the fact that he exists at all proves that the sprig of acacia, the promise of life and immortality, is somewhere within himself; and although the flame of life may appear faint or cold, if he will supply the fuel by his daily actions, he will kindle the altar flame once more within himself, which, shining forth, will also help his brother to kindle this flame, which is a living sacrifice to the living God.

Chapter II

The Sacred City *of* Shamballa

n every mythology and legendary religion of the world there is one spot that is sacred above all others to the great ideal of that religion. To the Norseman it was Valhalla, the City of the Slain, built of the spears of heroes, where feasting and warfare was the order of the day. Here the heroes fought all day and reveled by night. Every day they killed the wild boar and feasted on it, and the next day it came to life again. In the Northland they tell that Valhalla was high on the top of the mountains, and that it was connected to the earth below by Befrost, the Rainbow Bridge; that up and down this bridge the Gods came, and Odin, the All-father, came down from Asgard, the City of the Gods, and worked and labored with mankind.

Among the Greeks, Mount Olympus was held sacred, and here the gods are said to have lived high on the top of a mountain. The Knights of the Grail are said to have had their castle among the crags and peaks of Northern Spain on Mount Salvart. In every religion of the world there is a sacred spot: Meru of the oriental, and Mount Moriah and Mount Sinai (upon which the tablets of law were given to man); all those are symbols of one universal ideal, and as each of these religions claimed among the clouds a castle and a home, so it is said that all the religions of the world have their headquarters in Shamballa, the Sacred City in the Gobi Desert of Mongolia.

Among the oriental peoples there are wonderful legends of this sacred city, where it is said the Great White Lodge or Brotherhood meets to carry on the governing of world affairs. As the Assirs of Scandinavia were twelve in number, as Olympus had twelve gods, so the Great White Brotherhood is said to have twelve members, which meet in Shamballa and direct the affairs of men. It is said that this center of universal religion descended upon the earth when the polar cap, which was the first part of the earth to crystallize, became solid enough to support life. Science now knows that not only does the earth have two motions, that of rotation upon its axis and revolution around the sun, but that it has nine other motions, according to Flammarion, the French astronomer. One of these motions is that of the alternation of the poles; in other words, some day that part of the earth's surface which is now the North Pole will become the South Pole. Therefore, it is said that the Sacred City has left its central position and after much wandering is now located in Mongolia.

Those who are acquainted with the Mohammedan religion will see something of great interest in the pilgrimage to the Kabba at Mecca, where thousands go each year to give honor to the Stone of Abraham, the great aerolight, upon which Mohammed is said to have rested his foot. Old and young alike, some even carried, wind through desert sands and endure untold hardships, many coming from great distances, to visit the place they cherish and love. In India we find the same thing. There are many sacred places to which pilgrims go, even as the Templars went in our Christian religion to the Sepulcher of Christ. Few see in this anything more than an outward symbol, but the true student recognizes the great esoteric truth contained therein. The spiritual consciousness in man is a pilgrim on the way to Mecca. As this consciousness passes upward through the centers and nerves of the body, it is like the pilgrim, climbing the heights of Sinai, or the Knight of the Grail returning to Mount Salvart.

When the spinal fire of man starts upward in its wanderings, it stops at many shrines and visits many holy places, for like the Masonic brother and his Jacob's Ladder, the way that leads to heaven is upward and inward. The spinal fire goes through the centers or seed ground of many great principles, and worships at the shrine of many Divine Essences within itself, but it is eternally going upward, and finally it reaches the great desert. Only after pain and suffering and long labor does it cross that waste of sand. This is the Gethsemane of the higher man, but finally he crosses the sacred desert, and before him in the heart of the Lotus rises the Golden City, Shamballa.

The Lotus:
May your consciousness be lifted upward through the Tree of Life
within yourself until in the brain it blossoms forth as the Lotus,
that rising from the darkness of the lower world,
lifts its flower to catch the rays of the Sun.

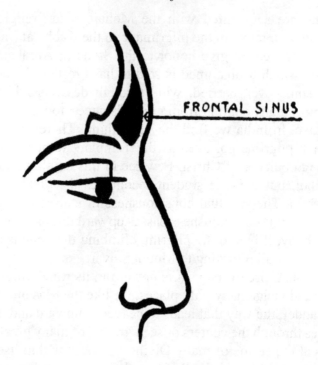

FRONTAL SINUS

In the spreading of the bone between the eyes called the frontal sinus, is the seat of the divine in man. There, in a peculiar gaseous material, floats, or rather exists, or is, the fine essence which we know as the Spirit. This is the Lost City in the Sacred Desert, connected to the lower world by the Rainbow Bridge, or the Silver Cord, and it is to this point in himself that the student is striving to rise. This is the Sacred Pilgrimage of the Soul, in which the individual leaves the lower man and the world below and climbs upward into the Higher Man or Higher World, the brain. This is the great pilgrimage to Shamballa, and as that great city is the center for the direction of our earth, so the corresponding great city in man is the center for his governmental system.

When any other thing governs man, he is not attuned to his own higher self, and it is only when the gods, representing the higher principle, come down the Rainbow Bridge and labor with him, teaching him the arts and sciences, that he is truly receiving his divine birthright. In the Orient the student looks forward with eager longing to the time when he shall be allowed to worship before the gates of the sacred city; when he also shall see the Initiates in silent conclave around the circular table of the zodiac; when the veil of Isis shall be torn away, and the cover lifted from the Grail Cup.

The Rod That Budded:

The buds in the Rod are the seven centers within yourself, which when you develop their spiritual powers shine out as centers of fire within your own being. The ancients have taken flowers to symbolize these centers, which when they shine out show that the dead stick, cut from the Tree of Life, has budded.

Let the student remember that all of these things must first happen within himself before he can find them in the universe without. The twelve Elder Brothers within himself must first be reached and understood before those of the universe can be comprehended. If he would find the great Initiates without, he must first find them within; and if he would see that Sacred City in the Lotus Blossom, he must first open that Lotus within himself, which he does, petal by petal, when he purifies and attunes himself to the higher principles within. The Lotus is the spinal column once more; its roots, deep in materiality; its blossom, the brain; and only when he sends upward nourishment and power, can that Lotus blossom within himself— blossom forth with its many petals, giving out their spiritual fragrance.

Sometimes you will see in store windows funny little Chinese gods or oriental Buddhas sitting on the blossom of a lotus. In fact, if you look carefully, you will find that nearly all of the oriental gods are so depicted. This means that they have opened within themselves that Spiritual Consciousness which they call the Shushuma. You have seen the funny little hats worn by the Hindu gods. They are made to represent a flower upside down, and once more, like the rod of Aaron that budded, we see the reference made to the unfolding of consciousness within. When the lotus blossom has reached maturity, it drops its seed, and from this seed new plants are produced. It is the same within the spiritual consciousness, which, when the plant is finished and its work is done, is released to work and produce other things.

In the Western World the lotus has been changed to the rose. The roses of the Rosicrucian, the roses of the Masonic degrees, and also those of the Order of the Garter in England, all stand for the same thing, the awakening of consciousness and the unfolding into full bloom of the soul qualities of man. When man awakens and opens this bud within himself, he finds, like the gold pollen in a flower, this wonderful spiritual city, Shamballa, in the heart of the lotus. When this pilgrimage of his spiritual fire is accomplished, he is liberated from the top of the mountain, as in the ascension of Christ, and the spiritual man, freed by his pilgrimage from the Wheel of Bondage, rises upward from among his disciples, the convolutions of the brain, with the great cry of the Initiate, which has sounded through the Mystery Schools for ages when the purified student goes onward and upward to become a pillar in the temple of his God. With that last cry the true mystery of Shamballa, the sacred city, is understood and he joins the ranks of those who in white robes of purity, their own soul bodies, gaze down upon the world and see others liberated in the same way, and who also sound the eternal tocsin, *"consumatum est"* (it is finished).

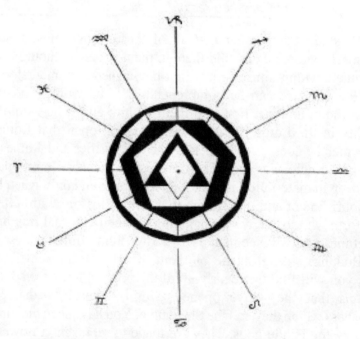

The Philosopher's Stone:

This is the true stone of the philosopher, which gives him power over all created things. This stone is himself. The experiences of his evolution have cut and polished the rough stone until in the Initiate it reflects the light of creation from a thousand different facets.

CHAPTER III

The Mystery *of the* Alchemist

 here are very few occult students today who have not heard of the alchemist, but there are very few who know anything about the strange men who lived during the Middle Ages and concealed under chemical symbolism the history of the soul. At a time, when to express a religious thought was to court annihilation at the stake or wheel, they labored silently in underground caves and cellars to learn the mysteries of nature which the religious opinions of their day denied them the privilege of doing. Let us picture the alchemist of old, deep in the study of natural lore. We find him among the test tubes and retorts of his hidden laboratory. Around him are massive tomes and books by ancient writers; he is a student of nature's mystery, and has devoted years, lives maybe, to the work he loves. His hair has long since grayed with age.

By the light of his little lamp he reads slowly and with difficulty the strange symbols on the pages before him. His mind is centered upon one thing, and that is the finding of the Philosopher's Stone. With all the chemicals at his command, their various combinations thoroughly understood, he is laboring with his furnace and his burners to make of the base metals the Philosopher's Gold. At last he finds the key and gives to the world the secret of the Philosopher's Gold and the Immortal Stone. Salt, sulfur, and mercury are the answer to his problem; from them he makes the Philosopher's Stone; from them he extracts the Elixir of Life; with the power that they give him he transmutes the base metals into gold. The world laughs at him, but he goes on in silence, really doing the things the world believes impossible.

After many years of labor, he takes his little lamp and silently slips away into the Great Unknown. No one knows what he has done, or the discoveries that he has made, but he, with his little lamp, still explores the mysteries of the universe. As the close of the fifteenth century clouded him with mystery, so the dawn of the twentieth century is crowning him with the glory of his just reward, for the world is beginning to realize the truths he knew, and to marvel at the understanding which his years of labor had earned for him.

Man has been an alchemist from the time when he first raised himself, and with the powers long latent pronounced himself as human. Experiences are the chemicals of life which the philosopher is experimenting with. Nature is the great book whose secrets he seeks to understand through her own wondrous symbolism. His own Spiritual Flame is the lamp by which he reads, and without this the printed pages mean nothing to him. His own body is the furnace in which he prepares the Philosopher's Stone; his senses and organs are the test tubes, and incentive is the flame from the burner. Salt, sulphur, and mercury are the chemicals of his craft. According to the ancient philosophers, salt was of the earth earthy, sulphur was a fire which was spirit, while mercury was nothing, only a messenger like the winged Hermes of the Greeks. His color is purple, which is the blending of the red and the blue—the blue of the spirit and the red of the body.

The alchemist realizes that he himself is the Philosopher's Stone, and that this stone is made diamond-like when the salt and the sulphur, or the spirit and the body, are united through mercury, the link of mind. Man is the incarnated principle of mind as the animal is of emotion. He stands with one foot on the heavens and the other on the earth. His higher being is lifted to the celestial spheres, but the lower man ties him to matter. Now the philosopher, building his sacred stone, is doing so by harmonizing his spirit and his body. The result is the Philosopher's Stone. The hard knocks of life chip it away and facet it until it reflects lights from a million different angles.

The Five-Pointed Star:
This picture, known to all Masons, is that of the Soul. It is the Star of Bethlehem, which heralds the coming of the Christ within. The two clasped hands are the spirit and body united in the marriage of the Lamb. It is from the union of the higher with the lower that the Christ is born.

The Elixir of Life is once again the Spirit Fire, or rather the fuel which nourishes that fire, and the turning of the base metal into gold is accomplished when he transmutes the lower man into spiritual gold. This he does by study and love. Thus, he is building within himself the lost panacea for the world's woe. The turning of the base metal into gold can be called a literal fact, as the same chemical combination which spiritually produces gold, will also do this physically. It is a known fact that many of the ancient alchemists really did create the precious metal out of lead, alloy, etc. But it was upon the principle that all things contain some part of everything else; in other words, every grain of sand or drop of water has in some proportion every element of the universe therein. Therefore, the alchemist did not try to make something from nothing, but rather to extract and build that which already was, and this the student knows is the only possible course of procedure.

Man can create nothing from nothing, but he does contain within, in potential energy, all things; and like the alchemist with his metals, he is simply working with that which he already has. The living Philosopher's Stone is a very beautiful thing. Indeed, like the fire opal, it shines with a million different lights, changing with the mood of the wearer. The transmuting process, whereby the spiritual fire passing through the furnace of purification radiates from the body as the soul body of gold and blue, is a very beautiful one.

The Marriage of the Sun and Moon:
This takes place in man when the heart and mind are joined in eternal union.
It occurs when the positive and negative poles within are united,
and from that union is made the Philosopher's Stone.

The Masons have among their symbols that of a five-pointed star with two clasped hands within it, and in that we have the mystery of the Philosopher's Stone. The clasped hands represent the united man in which the higher and the lower are working for their mutual betterment, by a cooperative rather than a competitive system. The five-pointed star is the soul body, born of this co-operation; it is the living Philosopher's Stone, more precious than all the jewels of earth. From it pour the rivers of life spoken of in the Bible; it is the Star of the Morning that heralds the dawn of Mastery, and is the reward that comes to those who follow in the footsteps of the ancient alchemist.

It is well for the student to realize that the alchemy of life produces in natural sequence all of the states of progression which are explained in the writings of the alchemist, until finally the sun and the moon are united as described in the Hermetic Marriage, which is, in truth, the marriage of the body and the spirit for the mutual development of each other. We are the alchemists who centuries ago carried on in secret our studies of the soul, and we still have the same opportunity that we had then, even more than then, for now we can state our opinions with little danger of personal injury. The modern alchemist thus has an opportunity that his ancient brother never had. On a busy street corner he daily sees nature's experiments carried on. He sees the mixing of metals, and from the everyday book of life, through the power of analogy, he may study Divinity. Through experience and often suffering the steel of his spirit is tempered by the flame of life. As the moon in the zodiac touches off like a fuse the happenings of life, so his own desires and wishes touch off the powers of his soul, and the experiences may be transmuted into soul qualities when he has developed the eye which enables him to read the simplest of all books — everyday life.

The alchemist of today is not hidden in caves and cellars, studying alone, but as he goes on with his work, it is seen that walls are built around him, and while he is in the world, like the master of old, he is not of it. As he goes further in his work, the light of other people's advice and outside help grows weaker and weaker, until finally he stands alone in darkness, and then comes the time that he must use his own lamp, and the various experiments which he has carried on must be his guide. He must take the Elixir of Life which he has developed and with it fill the lamp of his spiritual consciousness, and holding that above his head, walk into the Great Unknown, where if he has been a good and faithful servant, he will learn of the alchemy of Divinity. Where now test tubes and bottles are his implements, then worlds and globes he will study, and as a silent watcher will learn from that Divine One, who is the Great Alchemist of all the universe, the greatest alchemy of all, the creation of life, the maintenance of form, and the building of worlds.

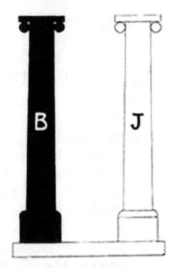

The Pillars of the Temple:
These pillars symbolize the heart and mind, the positive and the negative poles of life. Those who would enter the temple must pass BETWEEN the pillars. Every extreme is dangerous. It is the point between all poles that is safe to stand upon. You cannot enter the temple by the development of either the heart or mind alone, but only by the equal development of both.

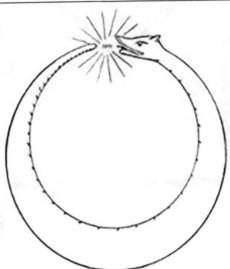

The Serpent:
This is the serpent crown of the ancient Gods. It shows that the two paths or parts of the spirit fire have been united. This crown is the symbol of mastery, and the union takes place within the student when the life forces are lifted to the brain.

Chapter IV

The Egyptian Initiate

 any ages have elapsed since the Egyptian Priest King passed through the pillars of Thebes. Ages before the sinking of Atlantis, thousands of years before the Christian Era, Egypt was a land of great truths. The hand of the Great White Brotherhood was held out to the Empire of the Nile, and the ancient pyramid passages resounded with the chants of the Initiates. It was then that the Pharaoh, now called half-human, half-divine, reigned in ancient Egypt. Pharaoh is the Egyptian word for king. Many of the later Pharaohs were degenerate and of little account. It is only the early Pharaohs we now list among the Priest Kings.

The Masonic Apron:
In the triangle we see spirit descending into the square of matter. Let us so purify matter that spirit may shine through it and make of us lights to guide the footsteps of humanity.

Try to picture for a moment the great Hall of Luxor—its inscriptive columns holding up domes of solid granite, each column carved with the histories of the gods. There at the upper end of the chamber sat the Pharaoh of the Nile in his robes of state; around him his counsellors, chief among them the priest of the temple. An imposing spectacle it was: the gigantic frame of the later Atlantean, robed in gold and priceless jewels; on his head the crown of the North and South, the double empire of the ancient; on his forehead the coiled serpent of the Initiate, the serpent which was raised in the wilderness that all who looked upon it might live; that sleeping serpent power in man, which coiled head downward around the tree of life, drove him from the garden of the Lord, but which raised upon the Cross, became the symbol of the Christ.

The Pharaoh was an Initiate of Scorpio, and the serpent is the transmuted Scorpio energy, which working upward in the regenerated individual is called the Kundalini. This serpent was the sign of Initiation. It meant that within him the serpent had been raised, for the true Pharaoh was a priest of God, as well as a master of men. There he sat upon the cube altar throne, indicating his mastery over the four elements of his physical body—a judge of the living and of the dead, who in spite of all his power and glory, having about him the grandeur of the world's greatest empire, still bowed in humble supplication to the will of the gods. In his hands he carries the triple sceptre of the Nile, the Shepherd's Crook, the Anubis-headed Staff and the Flail or Whip. These were the symbols of his work. They represent the powers which he had mastered. With the whip he had subjugated his physical body; with the Shepherd's Crook he was the guardian and keeper of his emotional body; with the Anubis-headed Staff he was master of his mind and worthy to wield the powers of government over others, because, first of all, he obeyed the laws himself.

With all his robes of state and with the scarab upon his breast, and with the All-seeing Eye above his throne, there was still nothing as precious or as sacred to the ancient Egyptian Priest King as the triangular girdle or apron which was the symbol of his initiation. The apron of the ancient Egyptian carried with it the same symbolism as the Masonic apron of today. It symbolized the purification of the bodies, when the seat of the lower emotions, Scorpio, was covered by the white sheepskin of purification. This symbol of his purification was the most precious belonging of the ancient Pharaoh; and this plain insignia, worn by many others below him in rank and dignity, but equal to him in spiritual purification, was the most precious of all things to the Priest King. There he sat, written upon him in the words of the Initiate, the symbols of his purification and mastery, a wise king of a wise people. And it was through these Priest Kings that the Divine worked, for they were of the order of Melchisedec. Through them was formed that doctrine which degeneracy has not been able to entirely obliterate, which we know as the divine right of kings—divine because through spirituality and growth God was able to manifest through them. They were conscious instruments in the hands of a ready writer, willing and proud to do the work of those with whom through knowledge and truth they had attuned themselves.

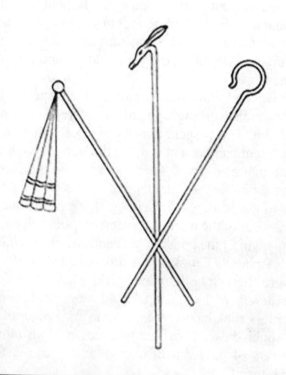

The Sceptres of Egypt:
These are the three bodies that are the tools with which we are to build our temple. When they are mastered, they are the living proof of our right to kingship.

But the time came, as in all nations, when selfishness and egotism entered the heart of king and people alike, and slowly the hand from the Great White Brotherhood that fed ancient Egypt was withdrawn, and the powers of darkness transformed the land of glory into one of ruins, and the names of mighty kings were buried beneath the oblivion of degeneracy. Mighty cataclysms shook the world, and out of the land of darkness the Great White Brotherhood carried the chosen people into the promised land; Egypt, the land of glory, disintegrated into dust.

The Sacred Scarab:
In this form the ancient Egyptians worshiped Khepera, the rising Sun, and the sacred scarab was buried with the dead as the symbol of resurrection. For as the sun rises from the darkness of night, so the divine spirit rises from the body that is no more. The life is eternal.

The great temples of the Pharaohs are ruins, and the temples of Isis are but broken heaps of sandstone. But what of the priest kings who labored there in the days of its glory? They are still with us, for those who were leaders before are leaders now, if they have continued to walk the path. Although his sceptre is gone, and his priestly vestments have moulded away, the Priest King still walks the earth with the dignity and the power and the childish simplicity that before made him great. He no longer wears the robes of his order. Although he bears no credentials, he is as much a priest king now as then, for he still bears the true insignia of his rank. The coiled serpent has given place to knowledge and love. The hand that bestowed the riches of the past does little acts of kindness now. Although he no longer carries the sceptres of self-mastery, still he manifests that mastery in his daily life. Although the altar fires within the temple at Karnac have long been dead, the true fire within himself still burns, and before that he still bows as he bowed in the days of Egypt's glory. Although the priest no longer is his counsellor, and the wise ones of his country no longer aid him in governmental problems, still he is never alone, for the priests in white and the counsellors in blue still march with him and whisper words of strength when he needs them.

Have you seen people that somehow you liked regardless of appearances? Have you seen other charming people whom you hated in spite of their charms? Have you seen learned people who were fools or impressed you as such, or people who knew little and yet you felt were wise? Those are the insignia of rank, which the loss of title or position cannot destroy. Kings with or without crowns they were—not puppets dressed in tawdry tinsel. And they still are kings and will be to the end of time, and they still manifest their rank, not by their superiority, and their high-headedness, but by the soul qualities which they radiate from themselves. The purity of their lives still radiates outward from those who wore the apron of the Initiate, for while that triangular apron with its serpent drawn upon it has long since rotted away, still the spiritual counterpart of that symbol radiates in their daily lives, proving beyond all dispute that they were Priest Kings and are today. We find them in every walk of life—in high places and down in the mire of life. But wherever we find them, they are still the mouthpieces of the gods, and through them comes the promise to all who strive. They are kings, not of the earth but of heaven, and in the life of our own Master we find one who joined himself to those who served, and was a true King even when his only crown was a wreath of thorns.

Still in the pyramid of Gizeh, the initiations continue; still the Initiate receives the insignia of his rank. Before that Fire within himself he makes his vows, and upon the burning altar of his own higher being he lays his crown and his sceptre, his robes and his diamonds, his hates and his fears, and sanctifies his life as a Priest King, and swears to serve none but his own higher self, the god within. His robes are his soul body; and his crown is his life, and in the streets of life he is enthroned. The dusky towers and factory chimneys around him fade into the templed pillars of Luxor, and with a lunch pail on his arm, his face brown with honest dirt, he is as much a king as when the crown of the double Nile rested upon his brow, and the priest of the temple made him one with his God and his fellowman.

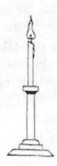

Chapter V

The Ark *of the* Covenant

ne of the most interesting symbols that has come down to us from the ancients is that of the Ark, or the box that was said to contain the sacred relics. Many people believe that this belongs particularly to the Jewish nation, but this is a great mistake, because it has been the birthright of every country to have the Ark. All have, like the Jewish people, lost much of their power and glory when they lost the sacred Ark. In ancient Chaldea and Phoenicia the Ark was well known. India celebrates it as the Lotus, and the ancient Egyptians tell how the moon god Osiris was imprisoned in an ark. In all the Mystery Religions of the world, individually and cosmically, the ark represents the fountainhead of wisdom. Over it the Shekinah's glory hovers, as a column of flames by night and a pillar of smoke by day. Every country has seen and felt its presence when the Priest Kings and Initiates bring out of an old civilization, lost because of crystallization, the sacred Ark, and surrounded by those faithful to the truth carry it into other lands and among other peoples.

In every creed and religion we find crystallization. We find small groups of people separating themselves from their brother man. We find those who, clinging to the old, refuse to advance with the new, and whenever we find this crystallization, we find the spirit of truth carried away to other people and embodied in other doctrines. The ancient Ark of the Israelite never had removed from it the staves by which it was carried and moved, until finally it was placed in Solomon's temple. Neither does the spirit fire in man rest until finally it is enthroned in the holy place of his solar temple. Ever towards the rising sun its bearers carry this sacred truth.

Nations are born of those who love the truth, and are buried when they forget it. The time has come when its silent bearers have taken the sacred Ark and the Shekinah's glory, and in solemn file have moved across the waters and brought it to the new world. The call has sounded through the universe, and those who are true to their own higher principles have surrounded the sacred chest. Those who have sworn alliance to their own higher being are following the priests and their sacred burden, and a beautiful mystery temple is being built in this beautiful land of ours, loved and guarded by those who are laboring for humanity. The staves are still in the Ark, however, and only when real good can be done by it will it remain.

The Priest before the Ark of the Covenant,
and the Spirit over the Mercy Seat.

The opportunity is now confronting the Western World. The knowledge of the ancients, the wisdom of the ages is knocking at the door and seeking those who will follow it. The bearers of the Ark have stopped and are gathering a nucleus of spiritual souls to carry on their work, and whether or not the word of the Lord will remain with a nation depends upon its own actions, and the actions of a nation are the collective actions of its individuals. If it finds nothing here attuned to itself, if it finds few that will answer to its call, the call of service and brotherhood, then will its priests lift again the staves and the sacred work will go out into other lands.

The life of a country thus gone, like the ancient city of the Golden Gate it will be swallowed up in oblivion. The call is sounding, and those who love the Truth and think and care for the Light must join that band of servers who have for centuries dedicated themselves to the preservation of Truth. Their lives they have given a thousand times, their happiness has been second to their duty. They are the keepers of the sacred Word, and the law of attraction draws to them all who love and live the Truth. A great influx of spiritual light comes to those who live the life and have learned the doctrine, and regardless of clan or country they have joined the silent file of watchers and workers around the sacred Ark of the Covenant. Every individual by his daily actions is expressing more plainly than by words his ideals, his desires, and his attitude towards this great work. The composite attitude of a certain number of people either shuts out or lets in the light. Therefore every individual has a great duty, a great work has to be done, and to that the true student must dedicate his life. Then wherever he may go, whatever he may do, he is being led, and the Shekinah's glory directs his footsteps.

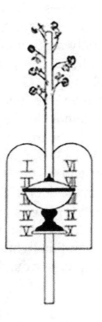

> ***The Rod that Budded, the Pot of Manna,***
> ***and the Tablets of the Law:***
> *In these three things contained within the Ark we see the*
> *threefold spirit contained within the ark of man's bodies.*

In the brain of man, between the wings of the kneeling cherubim, is the mercy seat, and there man speaks with his God as the priest of the tabernacle spoke to the spirit of the Lord hovering between the wings of the Angels. Man is again the Ark, and within him are the three principles, the Father, the Son, and the Holy Spirit—the tablets of the law, the pot of manna, and the rod that budded. But as in the case of the ancient Israelites, when they became crystallized the pot of manna and the rod that budded were removed from the Ark, and all that was left were the tablets or the letters of the law. When the individual crystallizes and excludes various sidelights from his mind, he excludes the life force which was flowing to him. In shutting out strangers, he shuts out his own life, and all that he has left are the tablets of the law, the material reasons from which the spiritual life has gone.

Solomon's temple, or the perfected temple of the human body, the perfected temple of the universe and the perfected temple of the soul, finally forms the perfect shrine for the living Ark. There at the head of a great cross it is placed, and there in man it becomes permanently fixed. The staves of polarity upon which it was carried are removed, and it becomes a living thing, a permanent place where man converses with his God. There man, the purified priest, arrayed in the robes of his order, the garments of his soul, converses with the spirit hovering over the Mercy Seat. This Ark within is always present, but man can only reach it after he has passed through the outer court of the Tabernacle, after he has passed through all the degrees of initiation, and after he has taken the Third Degree and becomes a Grand Master. Then and then only can he enter into the presence of his Lord, and there in the darkened chamber, lighted by the jewels of his own breast plate, he converses with the Most High, the true spiritual essence within himself.

We are working towards this, and the time will come when each person for himself will know the mystery of the Ark, when the student through purification shall be led through the door of the Holy of Holies and there be enveloped by the Light of Truth. This was his birthright which he sold for a mess of pottage. "To this end came he into the world that he might bear witness to this truth, that through this light all men might be saved." The Ark, that great spiritual principle, surrounded by its loving workers, is calling all to follow it.

When through materiality and degeneracy a great people are destroyed or a continent sinks beneath the ocean, then those that are true are called around the Ark, and as its faithful servers are led out of the land of darkness into the new world and a promised paradise. All great teachings set forth the same thing. The student will find that it is true, and when he allies himself with the powers of light, when he becomes a channel for its expression, and when he radiates it from himself to all who need it, then indeed will the Light protect him and he shall become a Sun of God.

The Holy Grail:
See in this cup your own body within which is the life blood of the Sun Spirit of the Universe. Each day that we live we perpetuate the Last Supper, and in all that we do we drink again the blood of Christ, the life power of the Cosmos.

Chapter VI

Knights *of the* Holy Grail

Before starting to take up the study of the Grail legends, it will be well for all who are interested to read those tales that are now listed under the heading of children's fairy stories. For example, the story of good King Arthur and his Round Table is a cosmic myth, and while there is little doubt that he as a man also lived, the real mystery as in the story of the Christ, is not the literal tale, but the great mystic or occult truth that it concealed under allegory and parable. It is the same with the story of Parsifal which can never be really understood and appreciated until the student sees in the Knight and later King of the Sacred Cup, his own spiritual development and the temptations he must also master if he would become a King of the Grail.

The Stone and the Sword:
Whoever can draw this sword from this stone is the master of the universe.

In Lohengrin also the same truth is shown to the world. It is the path of Initiation along which each must pass on his road to self-mastery. To every nation and in every tongue sacred legends have been given to teach man the path he must follow. The blind Homer of the Greeks who told of the wanderings of Ulysses gave the same great truths to the world. The Scalds of ancient Norway and Sweden and the Prophets of the Jews used the same means, and everywhere from the Sacred Books of the East to the legends of the American Indians we find one great connected truth told to many different people in ways that were best suited for their development.

Such a truth is the legend of the Round Table, given to King Arthur as a wedding gift. All true students know what wedding that was. Not of earth but the wedding of the Spiritual and Intellectual within the Initiate himself, when the spirit and the body are united eternally, each swearing to honor and protect the other. Of such a marriage was the union of Arthur and Guinevere in the legend of the King.

Let us first of all consider the coming of Arthur the King. We read in the legend of Arthur regarding Merlin the Magician, the wise man who it is said had charge of the coming King during his youth. Merlin represents the hand of the Elder Brothers, who realizing that a great ego had come into the world, had consecrated themselves to the work of preparing him for his mission.

The Rosicrucian Rose:
In this flower, which was painted upon the center of King Arthur's Table, we see the soul of man, which through purification and service has blossomed out with all the grandeur of the Initiate.

It was under the direction of Merlin, the master mind, that the anvil and stone with the sword thrust into it were raised in the square of the city when it became necessary for a new king to be selected. It was he also who called all of the brave knights of the country and told them that the one who could draw forth the sword would be king of all the land. And of all the knights in the land, Arthur the half-grown boy was the only one who could release the sword.

There is a very wonderful mystery of the soul contained within that divine allegory. Let us read the letters that were engraved upon the sword. "WHO SO PULLETH OUT THIS SWORD OF THIS STONE AND ANVIL IS RIGHT-WISE KING BORN OF ENGLAND."

The cube stone is the body; it has been so symbolized for centuries, and today among the Masons the Ashler is the symbol of Man. Experience is the anvil, and it is upon this anvil that the sword is tempered. The sword is spirit, and he who would be King in the true spiritual sense of the word must first show his divine power by freeing the Sword of Spirit from the casings of the lower man and the world.

It is the same symbol as that later used by Sir Galahad, the guileless knight, the personification of the purified man, who comes without a sword but who later arms himself with the sword of spirit that he draws from the cube block which was floating down the river (of life) past Camelot. Sir Galahad had the strength of ten because his heart was pure, and the Knight of today must follow in the same path.

The Sacred Spear:
*This is the spear of Passion that pierces the side of the Christ,
the higher principle in man. But when in the hand of the pure of heart
this power can heal the very wound it caused.*

If you have read the story of King Arthur, you will remember how he was given Excalibur, the enchanted sword, how it came up out of the water held by a hand draped in white. Excalibur represents light and truth, which is the weapon of the true Initiate.

In England there still hangs on a courthouse wall the Round Table of King Arthur. In the very center of the table is a beautiful rose painted in natural colors. This symbol is that of the Rosicrucians, the ancient alchemists, and there is a direct connection between the legend of the British King and the ancient philosophers of fire.

Now let us turn our attention for a moment to the history of the Holy Grail, or the cup from which Christ drank at the Last Supper and which was said to have caught his blood when he was dying upon the cross. Ancient legends tell us that this cup was made from a sacred stone which had been the crown jewel of Lucifer, the dynamic energy of the universe. It was said that the green stone had been struck from the crown of Lucifer by the archangel Michael during the famous battle in heaven.

After the death of Christ it is said that Joseph of Arimathea took the sacred cup and the spear of the Passion and carried them into a distant land. He wandered with his sacred relics through Europe and is said to have finally died, and those who came after him after many centuries of tribulation carried the sacred relics to Mount Salvart in northern Spain where they remained until Parsifal finally took the grail and spear back to the East where it is to be now preserved.

It is around this cup and spear that the legends of Parsifal and King Arthur have been written, and it is through study of this fact that we are able to better understand the mystery of the Great White Lodge of which the Round Table of Arthur and the circular temple of the knights of the Grail is a symbol.

Although we no longer have the cup as a physical symbol, it is not gone from among us, and as in the days of old the brave knights of the Round Table went out to fight for right, so those knights of today who belong to the Great White Brotherhood go out into the world in the name of truth and labor with mankind and seek to right the wrongs of the world. It is said that the knights of Arthur's court always fought for virtue and purity, and so did those who rode out of Mount Salvart.

The grail cup is the symbol of the creative force of nature; it is also the symbol of the human race which is slowly learning the mysteries of creation. Within the cup is the blood of Christ, that force which is transmuting the body into soul, fast or slowly as we give it greater or lesser opportunity.

In the sacred spear we find symbolized again the creative force, which in the hands of Klingsor, the evil one, wounds and causes suffering, but which when held by the pure Parsifal heals the very wound that it caused.

A great lesson is being taught to man through these allegories, but the average person is unwilling to stop and consider them. They do not realize that they themselves are the ones whom the Elder Brothers of humanity must use in the fight against the forces of evil. They do not realize that the dragons and ogres of the legends are their own lower natures which they must overcome. They do not see in the hand-to-hand combat of the knights of old for a lady's hand the higher and lower man fighting for the soul within.

The knight of today does not realize that the white armor that he wears is his own purified body which is proof against all the attacks of vice and passion, but nevertheless this is the meaning of the legend. His shield is truth, which is a perfect protection to the inner man. His strong right arm is the knowledge and spiritual power he has developed within, and the sword that he uses is the spiritual light with which the pure flame of the spirit fire dispels the darkness of ignorance and the demons of lust.

The sacred spear and the cup which he serves are the two poles of the creative life force within, the development of which he gains as he daily serves his fellow men.

Far from the uninitiated the twelve Elder Brothers of mankind sitting around the circular table of the universe watch the knights in their battle of life, and the time comes when the student having finished his work here is liberated at the foot of the Grail. There the candidate stands robed from head to foot in the armor of spirit and in the pure white of a body that has been cleansed. Then the cloth is lifted from the sacred cup, and he is illuminated by the light which would have killed him had he seen it without purification. He then takes his place among the knights of the Round Table, and joins those who give up all and labor for humanity.

When in sickness and in suffering we beg of the great unknown that he send us help, then indeed our knight comes to us as Lohengrin came to Elsa. When our loved ones pass into the great unknown, there stands the brother of the Grail, the invisible helper, who through days of labor has earned the right to become a member of that great band of servers who gather around the table of the King, and while their bodies are asleep still labor in their great search for light and truth, and pray for the day when they shall also become Kings of the Holy Grail.

Chapter VII

The Mystery *of the* Pyramid

here comes a time in the development of the occult student when he understands one of the great secrets of the Initiates, and that is that every sacred thing outside of himself stands for some organ or function within himself. This is, of course, true in the case of the Great Pyramid, except that this particular pile of stone said by many to be the oldest building on the surface of the earth, is the great symbol of composite man. In other words, it stands for man as a unit.

Let us first consider it simply from the exterior standpoint. When we first look at it in the distance it seems to be one great stone, but as we come closer we see that it is made of thousands of smaller stones, each one carefully fitted into place. Here we see the first likeness between the pyramid and man. We consider man to be a unit, but when we examine more closely, we find that he is a great number of small units, each working in harmony with the others. It is the same with everything. We take a successful life, and we think of it as an entirety, but when we examine it, we find that it is a number of small achievements joined together.

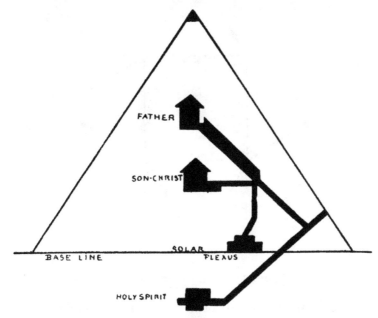

Cross Section of the Great Pyramid of Gizah

As thousands of workmen were used in the building of the pyramid, so there are unnumbered workmen at work in the building of our bodies, which are symbolical of the same building.

There are many pyramids all over the world. We find them in South America and in Mexico; we find mounds which were made to represent them among the American Indians, and in Europe and Britain we find remnants of the same things. But there is only one real pyramid in all the world. Even the others in Egypt are but copies of the Great Pyramid, and were used as tombs for the Pharaohs, but nobody was ever found in Cheops, nor were there ever any signs that it had been so used.

Now let us continue our analogy between the pyramid and man. If you will look at the accompanying illustration, you will see the pyramid laid flat, and you will notice it is made of four triangles laid around the base square. The four-sided base of the pyramid represents the four elements of which man's bodies are composed. These are hydrogen, nitrogen, oxygen and carbon, or earth, water, fire, and air. These are called the base of all things, and upon this base the four bodies of man are raised, each from its own element. Thus, the physical body is raised from the earth. The vital body is raised from the water, the emotional body from the fire, and the mental body from the air.

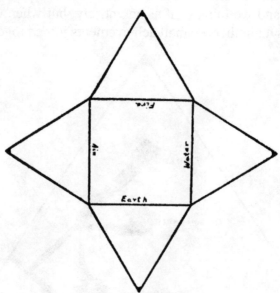

The Pyramid – Earth, Water, Fire and Air

Here we see the pyramid laid out so that the four triangles and the square are clearly seen. This represents man once again, and the ancient Pyramid is man offering his higher being upon the altar of the Great Fire Spirit.

There are twelve lines used in the drawing of the four triangles, which stand for the twelvefold constitution of man when it is complete: the threefold body, the threefold mind, the threefold soul, and the threefold spirit. It also gives us the twelve signs of the zodiac, divided into their respective groups.

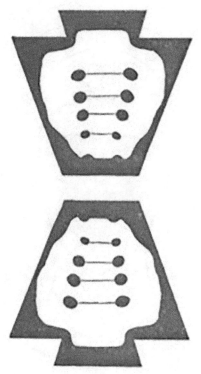

Out on the desert stands the Sphinx, the Guardian of the Threshold mentioned by Bulwer Lytton. It stands for the bodies of man, and is that strange being which must be passed before the student can go on in his development. The four fixed signs of which the Sphinx is a symbol are Taurus the Bull, Leo the Lion, Scorpio the Eagle, and Aquarius the Man, or the human head.

I have already given you some work on the sacrum bone, and I told you that it was the gravedigger's spade. Here is a picture of the head of the Sphinx, and the inverted sacrum bone when it has been turned upward. We see the Sphinx in the inverted sacrum and also in it the inverted Masonic keystone. All this is very interesting, but unless we realize the inner meaning of it, its true value is lost. But it is not chance that these things should be so.

You have most of you heard of the Dweller on the Threshold, that creature built by our own actions and mistakes. Well out on Egypt's desert it stands and bars the way to the pyramid, the temple of the higher man. And the message that it gives to the world is:

"I am the bodies. If you would go on to the temple you must master me, for I am within you."

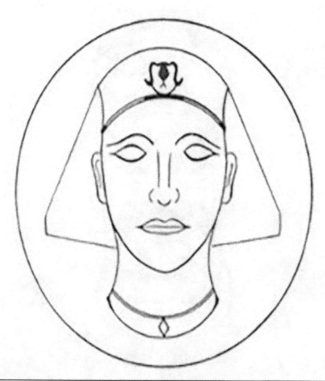

The Sphinx:
This is that mysterious being suspended 'twixt heaven and earth,
which has the head of a human being and the body of an animal.
In other words the Sphinx symbolizes man.

The Sphinx again symbolizes man, with the mind and spirit of the human rising out of the animal desires and emotions. It is the riddle of the ages, and man is once more the answer.

It is said that in ancient times the Sphinx was the gateway of the pyramid, and that there was an underground passage which led from the Sphinx to Cheops. This would make the symbolism even more perfect, for the gateway to the spirit is through the bodies according to the ancients.

Let us now enter the pyramid and passing through the corridors come to the King's Chamber as it is called. There are three great rooms in the pyramid which are of great interest to the student. The highest is the King's Chamber, then below that is the Queen's Chamber, and down below the surface of the earth is the Pit. Here we again find the great correlation between the pyramid and man. The three rooms are the three great divisions in man which are the seats of the threefold spirit. The lower room is the generative system under the control of Jehovah. The center room or Queen's Chamber is the heart, under the control of the Christ; and the upper room or the King's Chamber is the brain, which is under the control of the Father. In this upper room is the coffer made of stone, the meaning of which has never been explained, but which the student recognizes as the third ventricle in the brain.

It is quite certain also that this coffer was used as a tomb during initiation, when as is the case in the Masonic initiations of today, (which are the remnants of the ancient mysteries) the candidate was buried in the earth and resurrected, a symbol of the death of the lower man and the liberation of the higher.

It is said that Moses was initiated in the Great Pyramid, and some also say that Jesus was instructed there also. Be that as it may, we know that for thousands of years since the time it was built by the Atlanteans it has been the greatest temple of Initiation in the world. It seems also that its work is not yet done, for mutely it is teaching those who will see the mysteries of creation.

It is said by many that it is the original Solomon's Temple, but this we know is not true, for while it may be the first and original material temple, the true temple of Solomon is the universe, the Solarman's temple, which is slowly being rebuilt in man as the temple of the Soul of Man.

There is probably no point that is as important in connection with the pyramid as that of the corner stone. On the very top of the great pyramid is a comparatively flat place about thirty feet square. In other words, the TRUE STONE WHICH IS THE HEAD OF ALL THE CORNERS IS MISSING. If we look at the reverse side of the United States seal, we find again the pyramid from which the top is separated. Omar Khayyam, the Persian Poet, gives us the secret of the keystone when he says:

*"From my base metal shall be filed a **key**,*
Which shall unlock the door he howls without."

The value of the stone is better understood when you understand that it completes all of the triangles at once, and without it none of them are complete.

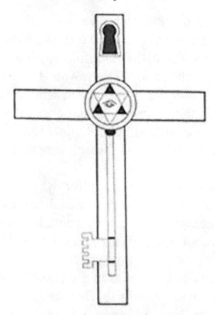

The Key and the Cross:
Upon the cross of matter that forms our bodies, hangs the key to all the mysteries of creation. It is our duty to take this key and with it unlock the door that conceals from us the unknown. This key is the spirit. Release it.

This stone is the spirit in man, which fell from its high position, and has been lost beneath the rubbish of the lower man. This is the true cap stone that is now hidden in the pit of man's temple, and which he must exhume and place again as the true crown of his spiritual pyramid.

He can only do this when he calls the thousands of workmen within himself together and binds them to the service of the higher man. There must be no traitors to murder the builder this time. And Lucifer, the one rejected by man as the devil, is the one who must through the planet Mars send man the dynamic energy which man himself must transmute from the fire of passion to the flame of spirit. He then must take the tools of the craft and cut and polish his own being into the cap stone of the Universal Temple.

It is interesting to note how the casing stones that once made the pyramid so beautiful and true were carried away to build the cities nearby, and in connection with that it is interesting to note how the soul and body of man, the casing stones of his spiritual temple, have been sacrificed in order that he might have material things.

As we look at pictures of the ancient pyramid and Sphinx which have stood on Egypt's sands for ages, let us see in them our own mystery temple, made without the sound of hammer or the voice of workman. And as we sadly think of this mighty ruin, broken by ages of neglect, let us remember our temple, and that its corner stone is missing also, and our walls are falling with neglect. Let us learn the lesson which it teaches, hasten to perfect our pyramid, cap it with the stone of spirit, offer upon its altars our sacrifice to the Great Sun Spirit, and bury our lower nature in its ancient coffer. Then for us will its mysteries be revealed, and the sealed lips of the Sphinx give up their secret.

WHERE YOUR
TREASURE IS,
THERE WILL YOUR
HEART BE ALSO.

THE WHITE GRAIL

Choose now your path

Service.

Self-Sacrifice.

Purification.

Love.

Study.

THE BLACK GRAIL

Choose now your path

Prosperity at others expense.

Selfishness.

Short-cuts.

Mastered by appetite.

Comfort.

FINIS